WELCOME TO EDINBURGH CASTLE

Mighty Edinburgh Castle dominates its city like no other castle in Europe. For 3,000 years, humans have sought safety on the Castle Rock. In ancient times they called it Din Eidyn, 'the stronghold of Eidyn'. Then, around AD 638, the Angles invaded, and ever since the rock has been known by its English name – Edinburgh.

In the Middle Ages, Edinburgh became Scotland's chief royal castle, enduring siege after siege during the long wars with England. By the time of King James VI's birth here in 1566, the castle was little more than a garrison fortress. The Jacobite siege in 1745 proved to be the last. Since that time, the ancient castle has found a new role as a national icon, a major visitor attraction and a World Heritage Site. But the garrison of soldiers remains.

Above: The Scottish Royal Arms as they appear in the Royal Palace.

Opposite: Mons Meg, the medieval siege cannon, presented to King James II in 1457.

CONTENTS

EDINBURGH CASTLE AT A GLANCE

This tour begins at the Portcullis Gate, the old ceremonial entrance to the castle, and progresses upwards to the summit of Castle Rock, 134m above sea level. At the top stands St Margaret's Chapel, the oldest building in the castle – and in Edinburgh. Close by is Crown Square, the heart of the royal castle, surrounded on all sides by imposing buildings, including the Royal Palace, the Great Hall and the Scottish National War Memorial. Thereafter, the tour takes you to places of interest on the castle's western side, including the Prisons of War exhibition, the Military Prison, and the exposed Western Defences.

Along the route are priceless treasures – the giant medieval gun Mons Meg, the Honours of Scotland – the oldest crown jewels in the British Isles – and the Stone of Destiny, Scotland's ancient Coronation Stone. There are also military museums for two of Britain's oldest regiments, as well as the National War Museum. At almost every step, there are spectacular views over Scotland's capital city and the country around. There are also gift shops and cafés. And if you're visiting at lunchtime, you can see and hear the famous One o' Clock Gun being fired.

Opposite: Edinburgh Castle seen from Princes Street.

DEFENDER OF THE NATION

46 AN ANCIENT FORTRESS
The Castle Rock is the oldest continuously occupied fortified place in Britain.

8 ARTILLERY DEFENCES
The castle is protected by ranks of cannon batteries, and is home to the huge medieval siege gun Mons Meg.

12/16 MILITARY MUSEUMS
The proud history of Scotland's regiments is celebrated at three museums within the castle.

HOME OF ROYALTY

28 THE ROYAL PALACE
The imposing residence of Scotland's royal family, where Mary Queen of Scots gave birth to James, the future king of both Scotland and England.

32 THE GREAT HALL
The castle's main ceremonial space, whose original, early-16th-century hammerbeam roof survives.

18 ST MARGARET'S CHAPEL
The oldest building in Edinburgh was built around 1130 by David I and dedicated to his mother.

HEART OF SCOTLAND

SPECTACULAR MONUMENT

Toilets

Castle Shop

Cafe/Restaurant

Visitor Information

Audio Guide
collection point

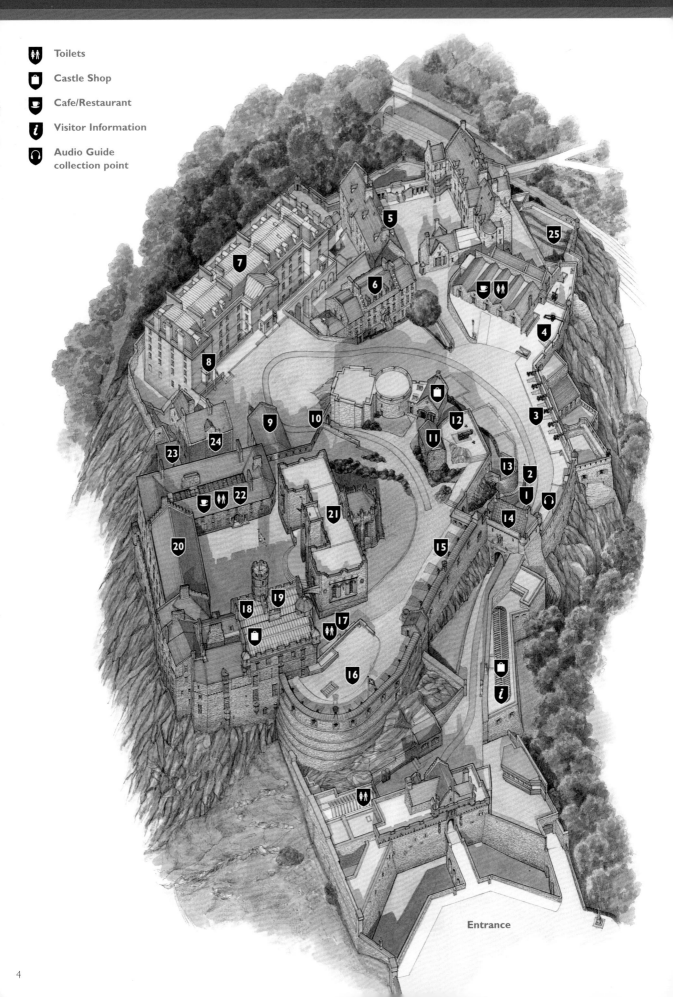

Entrance

Above: George III rainhead on the Governor's House.

Above: The Scottish Royal Arms as represented on the Gatehouse.

Above: St Andrew in stained glass in St Margaret's Chapel.

Above: Displays of antique weaponry in the Great Hall.

Illustration key

A GUIDED TOUR

Edinburgh Castle has played many roles over many centuries. It has been a residence for Scotland's monarchs, a prison for her enemies, a repository for her treasures – but it has always been a military stronghold. To this day, the Army has a military and ceremonial presence here.

Built on steep volcanic rock, the castle is naturally well defended. Although it was captured and recaptured several times during the Wars of Independence with England, and greatly damaged during the 16th-century Lang Siege, it still retains important structures from its medieval past. These include St Margaret's Chapel, the most ancient building in Edinburgh, dating from the 12th century; David's Tower, built in the 14th century as the royal residence of Robert the Bruce's son David II; and the Royal Palace and Great Hall, constructed in the 15th and early 16th centuries.

This tour will guide you through the castle, describing its buildings, its treasures and its other key features, and explain how each development was prompted by its changing role. Guided tours are also provided free of charge by well-informed castle stewards; and audio guides are available for hire.

The castle's major points of interest are signposted with numbered shield symbols. These correspond with the numbers given on the orientation drawing and throughout this guided tour. Numbers above 25 refer only to the audio-guided tour.

The second half of this book tells the history of the castle in more detail, describing some of the episodes that helped shape the nation. Welcome to a castle at the very heart of Scotland's history and identity.

1 THE CASTLE GATES

The eastern side of the castle has always been the main approach to the mighty Castle Rock. Compared with the other three sides, which are steep, dangerous crags, this approach was relatively easy to climb. But this also made it vulnerable. Consequently, it has seen remarkable change over the centuries.

THE PORTCULLIS GATE

You have just passed through the fortified archway known as the Portcullis Gate. This formidable entrance was built as the principal gateway into the castle after the Lang Siege ended in 1573. It originally had four barriers – an iron portcullis and three pairs of wooden doors. You can still see the iron crooks on which the heavy doors were hung.

Above: A plaque commemorates the daring raid by which the castle was seized back from the English during the Wars of Independence.

Opposite: The formidable Portcullis Gate, installed in the late 16th century.

2 THE LANG STAIRS

Next to the Portcullis Gate is a steep flight of 70 steps, aptly named the Lang Stairs. This was the main way up to the summit in medieval times. The stairs once passed beneath the lofty Constable's Tower, which was destroyed in the Lang Siege; the curved wall on the right as you climb up may have formed part of that tower. A plaque high up on the wall commemorates the successful assault on the castle by Sir Thomas Randolph, Earl of Moray, in 1314, during the Wars of Independence with England. The date of 1313 given on the plaque is inaccurate.

Rather than struggling up the Lang Stairs, why not take the curved cobbled road ahead, a more leisurely route to the summit? This approach was formed in the 17th century to ease the movement of heavy guns in and out of the castle. The central strip of small granite pieces provided better grip for the horses' hooves.

Left: The Lang Stairs were once the main route to the heart of the castle.

3 THE ARGYLE BATTERY

This six-gun battery, opposite the Lang Stairs, was built in the 1730s. It was named after John Campbell, 2nd Duke of Argyll, who defeated the Jacobites at Sheriffmuir in 1715. The battery was built on the orders of Major-General George Wade, better known for his military roads in the Scottish Highlands. It was designed by Captain John Romer, a military engineer, better known for designing mighty Fort Augustus, and built by William Adam, better known for designing great country houses but here working as a building contractor.

The guns are not the original armament but on loan from the Royal Armouries. They are cast-iron, muzzle-loading 18-pounders, made around 1810, the time of the Napoleonic Wars with France. The royal cipher GR3 (for King George III) appears on the top of each barrel.

THE CARTSHED

Just beyond the Argyle Battery is an 18th-century building which now houses the Redcoat Café. It was built as a Cartshed in 1746, following the Battle of Culloden, which ended the fifth and final Jacobite Rising. By this date, the castle was crammed with soldiers, and the structure, originally open-fronted, held 50 carts that brought provisions up from the town to the garrison.

Above: The cannon that line the Argyle Battery date from the early 19th century.

Below left: The 18th-century Cartshed was originally used to store carts delivering goods to the garrison.

Below right: The One o'Clock Gun is fired six days a week by the gunkeeper, Sergeant James Shannon 'the Cannon'.

'The third day the gun boomed out at one o'clock exactly, frightening the citizens and scattering the flocks of pigeons roosting on the city's buildings.'

Account of the first firing (after two failed attempts) on 7 June 1861.

4 THE ONE O'CLOCK GUN

On Mills Mount Battery, to the right of the Cartshed, stands the One o'Clock Gun. It is fired every day (except Sundays, Good Friday and Christmas Day) at 1300 hours. The citizens of Edinburgh check their watches; visitors jump out of their skins! The gun was originally suggested by John Hewitt, an Edinburgh businessman, who had seen a similar time-gun in Paris in 1846. His idea bore fruit when a time-ball was added to the top of the Nelson Monument, the telescope-shaped building on Calton Hill, as a visual signal for shipping in the Firth of Forth. Hewitt's proposal, that this could be accompanied by an audible signal, was then taken up, and in June 1861 the first firing took place from Edinburgh Castle. It has continued uninterrupted ever since, except for periods during the two World Wars.

The present gun is a 105mm field gun, installed in 2001.

THE LOW DEFENCES

Via a staircase on Mills Mount Battery you can access the Low Defences, directly below the Argyle Battery. From this two-gun battery you can enjoy an uninterrupted view over the city.

VIEWS FROM THE CASTLE

Main image

The views from the battlements are outstanding – unless you are visiting when the thick sea mist, called the 'haar', rolls in. Dramatic views to the west, south and east can be seen from other parts of the castle, but the view north in particular is among the most spectacular in Scotland. Spread out before you is the 18th-century New Town, one of the greatest works of Georgian town-planning in the British Isles. Beyond it you can see the Firth of Forth, with its little islands dotted about, and the famous Forth Bridges. In the distance can be seen numerous mountain peaks – among them Ben Lomond.

3 North view

The Argyle Battery looks out over Princes Street and the New Town and across the Firth of Forth. In good weather, Fife is clearly visible beyond the water.

THANK YOU FOR VISITING

Edinburgh Castle
Castle Hill
Edinburgh, Scotland
Tel: 0131 225 9846

Save money on shop, gobstore

Stretching with an Explorer Pass

For more information visit

QTY PLU	DESCRIPTION	AMOUNT
1 9781904	Souvenir Guide E	4.45
1 1	ADULT	11.90
1 1	ADULT	11.90

TOTAL Inc VAT	
VAT at 17.5%	
TOTAL	
POUNDS	
CHANGE	0.00

7060

:36   16/06/2010   001:117060   144

Thank you for visiting Edinburgh Castle

CASTLE

Thank you for visiting Edinburgh Castle.
Save money on entry to other
attractions with an Explorer Pass.

For more information visit:
www.edinburghcastle.gov.uk
or ask a member of staff for details.

EDINBURGH
CASTLE

Thank you for visiting Edinburgh Castle.
Save money on entry to other

Views: left to right

5 West view

The circular dome of the Usher Hall can be seen from the West Panorama, a raised walkway near the entrance to the National War Museum.

25 NW view

The Western Defences offer a good view of the domed roof of West Register House, with the Forth Rail Bridge just visible in the distance.

3 NE view

Looking to the right from the Argyle Battery, you can see across the dome of East Register House to Leith docks and Inchkeith island.

15 SW view

From St Margaret's Chapel there is a view across the city's residential Southside to the Pentland Hills.

5 THE NATIONAL WAR MUSEUM

In 1748, a gunpowder magazine capable of holding more than a thousand barrels was built on the sloping rock behind the Governor's House. It was soon joined by two ordnance storehouses, two-storey warehouses for cannon, small arms and other equipment. The magazine was demolished in 1897, but the ordnance storehouses were retained and converted for use as a military hospital. A mortuary was also built in Back Well Yard.

Above: Robert Gibb's famous painting, *The Thin Red Line* (1881), celebrates the two-man-deep battle formation used by the 93rd Highlanders at the Battle of Balaclava in 1854.

DID YOU KNOW…

On 16 October 1939 a German Luftwaffe bomber crash-landed near Edinburgh, following a raid on the Forth Rail Bridge. It was the first enemy aircraft to be shot down over Britain in the Second World War. The pilot was captured and held in the castle's military hospital.

These buildings remain, and are now occupied by the National War Museum, which opened in 1933 as the Scottish Naval and Military Museum. Its first home was in the Queen Anne Building. The impetus was the opening of the Scottish National War Memorial in 1927, and both were seen as a fitting and lasting tribute to the sacrifice made by Scottish men and women during the First World War. One in five Scots who enlisted in the armed services never made it home – a sobering statistic.

The museum's outstanding collection presents Scotland's military history from the creation of the first standing army in the 17th century to the present time. With a strong focus on the personal experience of military service across the world, themed exhibitions explore the impact of war on generations of the Scottish people. Highlights include 'Highland Soldier', the story of that unique military figure, and 'Active Service', looking at the nature of battle through the eyes of Scottish servicemen. The museum offers a military research library and a programme of special exhibitions.

Right: Lance Corporal Robertson of the 11th City of Edinburgh Battalion of the Home Guard, by Eric Kennington (1943).

Below: The building that now houses the National War Museum was built as an ordnance storehouse in the 18th century.

6 THE GOVERNOR'S HOUSE

The pleasing Georgian residence halfway up the hill from Mills Mount Battery was built in 1742 for the castle governor. Lodgings for his principal staff officers, the master gunner and storekeeper, were provided in the two wings. After the post of governor was abolished in 1860, nursing sisters from the castle hospital used the building. Today, it serves as an officers' mess and residence for the governor, a Crown appointment restored for purely ceremonial purposes in 1935. It is not normally open to visitors.

DID YOU KNOW…

The Governor's House is thought to have been the first home of the body that subsequently became the Ordnance Survey. In 1747, William Roy, a 20-year-old Lanarkshire lad based here in the castle, embarked on a military survey of Scotland for the Board of Ordnance. In later life, having risen to the rank of general, he established the mapping organisation we know as the Ordnance Survey. Roy's drawing office may have been in a basement room.

Below: The Governor's House is now an officers' mess for the garrison stationed in the castle.

7 THE NEW BARRACKS

Looming up behind the Governor's House is the enormous New Barracks, built during the wars with Napoleonic France. Work began in 1796, the year Napoleon married Josephine and swept through northern Italy. It was finished in 1799, the year the great general became undisputed leader of his country. The vast building housed an infantry battalion (600 officers and men).

It is not the most handsome structure in the castle. Sir Walter Scott likened it to 'a vulgar cotton mill', and his contemporary, Lord Cockburn, was overheard to say: 'Look on the west side of the castle – and shudder!'

The seven-storey building still serves a variety of military purposes. The only part normally open to visitors is the regimental museum of The Royal Scots Dragoon Guards (see page 16).

Above: The New Barracks was built to house more than 600 soldiers during the Napoleonic Wars of the late 18th century. The building still operates as a barracks.

THE REGIMENTAL MUSEUMS

I ndependent museums devoted to two of Scotland's oldest regiments are housed in the New Barracks and the Drill Hall opposite.

8 THE ROYAL SCOTS DRAGOON GUARDS MUSEUM

The Royal Scots Dragoon Guards (Carabiniers and Greys) was formed in 1971 through the amalgamation of two famous cavalry regiments – the 3rd Carabiniers and the Royal Scots Greys. The regiment's origins go back to 1678, when the Scots Greys were raised to help Charles II fight the Covenanters (religious dissenters). Their first battle was at Rullion Green, in the Pentland Hills on the southern outskirts of Edinburgh. Two Regiments of Horse, raised in 1685 and later designated Dragoon Guards, merged in 1922 to become the 3rd Carabiniers.

The museum tells the regiment's history from the bloody European wars of the 18th and 19th centuries to the global struggles of recent decades. Its most recent battle honours were awarded after the first Gulf War of 1991 and Iraq 2003. Pride among the many exhibits are the Eagle and Standard of the 45th French infantry, captured in 1815 during the epic opening charge of the Scots Greys at Waterloo, along with the sword of their captor, Sergeant Charles Ewart. The event is wonderfully captured in the painting 'The Fight for the Standard', which now hangs in the Great Hall. Ewart was later commissioned as Ensign and died in 1846. In 1938, his body was removed from its original grave in Salford to a tomb at the NW of the Esplanade.

Above: Richard Andsell's painting, which now hangs in the Great Hall, shows Sergeant Ewart seizing the Eagle.

Below left: The Imperial Eagle captured from Napoleon's 45th 'Invincibles' at the Battle of Waterloo in 1815.

'I saw Ewart, with five or six infantry men about him, slashing right and left … Ewart had finished two of them, and was in the act of striking a third man who held the Eagle; next moment I saw Ewart cut him down, and he fell dead … Almost single-handed, Ewart had captured the Imperial Eagle of the 45th "Invincibles".'

An eyewitness account of Waterloo by Scots Greys Corporal John Dickson, published in 1911.

45

9 THE ROYAL SCOTS MUSEUM

The Royal Scots (The Royal Regiment) is the oldest infantry regiment in the British Army. It was officially raised in 1633 by Sir John Hepburn to serve Louis XIII of France – with the blessing of King Charles I. In 1661, when Charles II was restored to the thrones of Scotland, England and Ireland, The Royal Scots too returned home to serve their king. The regiment is familiarly known as 'Pontius Pilate's Bodyguard' because of its seniority as the first British Infantry Regiment of the Line.

The museum tells the history of a regiment that was awarded its first battle honour at Tangier in 1680, and subsequently won another 148 around the world – taking part in Marlborough's campaigns in the early 18th century, Wellington's Peninsular War and the Battle of Waterloo, India, the Crimea, South Africa, two World Wars and campaign areas since.

In World War I the regiment expanded to 35 battalions, with over 11,000 killed and 40,000 wounded. The six Victoria Crosses won during that hideous conflict are on display.

Right: The Victoria Cross won by Private H.H. Robson for 'most conspicuous bravery' in Flanders on 14 December 1914. He was wounded twice while rescuing injured comrades.

Left to right:

A Royal Scots cartridge pouch dating from the late 19th century.

A souvenir tobacco tin from the Boer War.

Private H.H. Robson, V.C.

 FOOG'S GATE

Foog's Gate was built in the 17th century, during a major refortification of the castle commissioned by King Charles II. The origin of the name is unknown. In olden times it was 'Foggy Gate', referring perhaps to the 'haar', or thick sea mist that still shrouds the Castle Rock occasionally. The walls on both sides of the gate have openings for cannons and muskets.

Right: The mysteriously named Foog's Gate was added as part of a 17th-century refortification of the castle.

ST MARGARET'S CHAPEL

This tiny structure is the oldest building in the castle, indeed in Edinburgh. It was built around 1130 by David I as a private chapel for the royal family, and dedicated to his mother, Margaret. She died in the castle in 1093, devastated by the violent death of her husband, Malcolm III, in an ambush. It is possible that the chapel was originally part of a larger royal lodging, housing a hall and chambers, much like in Norman tower-keeps in England. The rubble masonry on the entrance side differs from the squared ashlar blocks around the other three sides.

Despite its very plain exterior, the chapel is delightfully decorated inside. A fine chevroned arch divides the small space into two: an apsidal chancel, housing the altar, and a rectangular nave for the royal family's use. The chapel was converted into a gunpowder store in the 16th century, and the stone-vaulted 'bomb-proof' ceiling dates from then.

Left: St Margaret herself is one of the subjects of the stained-glass windows. The others are St Andrew, St Ninian, St Columba and William Wallace.

The chapel's original function was rediscovered only in 1845, by the antiquarian Sir Daniel Wilson, who supervised its restoration. The stained-glass windows of St Andrew and St Ninian (in the chancel), St Columba, St Margaret and William Wallace were added in 1922 by Douglas Strachan, who later designed the windows in the Scottish National War Memorial.

The tiny space is still used as a picturesque setting for christenings and weddings. The furnishings are maintained by the ladies of the Guild of St Margaret in memory of their namesake, who died here in the castle over 900 years ago, and was canonised by Pope Innocent IV in 1250.

Above: Built around 1130, St Margaret's Chapel is the oldest building in Edinburgh.

Left: The interior features a fine chevroned arch. The stained glass was added in the 1920s.

12 MONS MEG

Mons Meg was presented to James II of Scotland in 1457, a gift from his niece's husband, Duke Philip of Burgundy. The six-tonne siege gun was then known simply as 'Mons' – after the Belgian town where she was made in 1449. She was at the leading edge of artillery technology, and fired gunstones weighing 330lbs (150kg).

Mons Meg was soon in action against the English, at the siege of Roxburgh Castle in 1460, in which James II lost his life. In 1497, James IV used her at the siege of Norham Castle, in Northumberland. Before this, he had her trundled over to Dumbarton Castle, on the Clyde, to teach the rebellious Earl of Lennox a lesson in loyalty.

But Mons Meg was very cumbersome. She could travel only three miles (5km) a day, hauled by a team of a hundred men. She ended her fighting days with James V's navy and was taken out of military service around 1550.

'Item, to certain pioneers for their labours in mounting Mons furth of her lair to be shot, and for finding and carrying her bullet frae Wardie Muir to the Castle'

From the *Accounts of the Lord High Treasurer* for 3 July 1558, recording expenditure incurred in firing Mons Meg to celebrate Mary Queen of Scots' wedding to the French Dauphin.

Thereafter, she was used as a saluting gun, famously fired in 1558 to celebrate the wedding of Mary Queen of Scots.

Mons Meg was last fired on 14 October 1681, in a birthday salute for the Duke of Albany (later James VII). Her barrel burst and she was dumped down near the Cartshed. There she lay until 1754, when she was taken to the Tower of London, a casualty of the Disarming Act that demilitarised Scotland after the Jacobite Risings. But her great bulk saved her from being melted down and 70 years later she was returned.

On 9 March 1829, a military escort accompanied her from the port of Leith to her place on the battlements. The most remarkable of all medieval guns, a symbol of Scotland's proud military past, Mons Meg had come home.

DID YOU KNOW…

Mons Meg had a range of almost two miles (3.2km). When she was fired in 1558, to celebrate Mary Queen of Scots' marriage to the French Dauphin, the gunstone was later found on Wardie Muir, where the Royal Botanic Garden is today.

13 THE DOG CEMETERY

The British are renowned for their love of dogs, and this little cemetery is proof. Since the 1840s it has served as a burial place for regimental mascots and officers' pet dogs. Here lie such 'faithfuls' as Jess, band pet of the 42nd Royal Highlanders (the Black Watch), who died in 1881, and Dobbler, who for nine years until his death in 1893 followed the Argyll and Sutherland Highlanders to such exotic locations as China, Sri Lanka and South Africa.

14 THE ARGYLE TOWER

The Argyle Tower is in effect the upper part of the Portcullis Gate, added to that ancient structure in 1887. It was designed by Hippolyte Blanc, an Edinburgh architect, and financed by the Edinburgh publisher, William Nelson, who hoped the tower might become the permanent home of the Honours of Scotland, the crown jewels. He died disappointed.

The tower is named after the 9th Earl of Argyll. He is said to have been imprisoned above the Portcullis Gate before his execution on 30 June 1685 for leading a rebellion against James VII. Argyll apparently dined well and slept soundly the night before his execution, and went to his death defiant to the end.

Above (top left): One of the graves at the Dog Cemetery.

Above: The Argyle Tower was added during a major redevelopment of the 1880s. It houses an exhibition showing other proposed restoration schemes of the Victorian era.

Opposite: The Forewall Battery. The iron basket was used as a warning beacon.

'CASTLES IN THE AIR'

By 1850 the castle was seen as a monument more than a fortress. The public wanted a 'proper' castle, not an assortment of Georgian military architecture. Proposals were invited to 'prettify' the place.

Robert Billings put forward a plan to build a new church on the site of the North Barracks, where the Scottish National War Memorial now stands, and Col. Richard Moody proposed an armoury in the form of a medieval keep, to the north of St Margaret's Chapel. Queen Victoria and Prince Albert, preparing to build their own fairytale castle at Balmoral, indicated approval, but nothing came of either scheme. Attention then moved to the much-hated New Barracks. Francis T. Dollman proposed to recast it in Scots Baronial style, but his plans were rejected.

He enjoyed more success with a fantastic vision for a French-style château in place of the ordnance storehouses and powder magazine (below). Work began in 1858 before being abandoned.

In 1864, David Bryce proposed a keep as a monument to Prince Albert: this scheme failed solely because Victoria wished such a memorial 'to stand by itself unconnected to any other work'.

15 THE FOREWALL BATTERY

The Forewall Battery was built in the 1540s, approximately on the line of the medieval defences. It was substantially reconstructed after the Lang Siege of 1571–3. It is now armed with cast-iron guns made during the wars with Napoleonic France.

DID YOU KNOW...

The iron basket on the Forewall Battery was used to raise the alarm in an emergency. In the 16th century, one lit beacon meant 'be on your guard'; four meant 'panic – the enemy [i.e. the English] are invading in strength'.

THE FORE WELL

The Fore Well was the castle's main water supply from the early 14th century. Although it is almost 34m deep, only the bottom three metres ever held water. This gave a capacity of just over 11,000 litres, barely enough to sustain a garrison in siege time. The well was abandoned in the 19th century when a piped water supply from the town was provided.

THE 'BLACK DINNER'

The first-floor hall of David's Tower was probably the scene for one of the most dastardly episodes in the castle's history – the 'Black Dinner' of 1440.

James II was just six years old when he succeeded his murdered father, James I, in 1437. Holding the reins of power was Sir William Crichton, Governor of Edinburgh Castle. Crichton soon exploited his powerful position to carry out a spectacular political assassination.

Crichton, arch-rival of the powerful Black Douglases, invited the 6th Earl of Douglas and his younger brother to dine with their young king in the castle. During the meal Crichton presented a bull's head to the earl 'which was a sign and token of condemnation to death'. James protested at this outrage, but to no avail. The Douglases were taken to an adjacent chamber and summarily tried on a trumped-up charge of treason. Swiftly found guilty, they were dragged out to the courtyard and beheaded.

16 THE HALF-MOON BATTERY

Above: The unique and imposing Half-Moon Battery was built in the late 16th century, to replace the ruined David's Tower.

Opposite: Little remains of the once formidable David's Tower, but visitors can explore part of the ruin.

Below: The royal seal of David II, who commissioned David's Tower in the 14th century.

The impressive curved wall of the Half-Moon Battery gives Edinburgh Castle an appearance unrivalled anywhere else in the world. It was built after the Lang Siege, over and around the ruin of David's Tower, to serve as the castle's chief high-level defence on its vulnerable east front. Following the 1689 siege it was repaired much as you see it now. Until 1716, the battery was armed with the famous 'Seven Sisters', bronze guns cast in the castle for James IV around 1500. The battery was also the first home of the One o'Clock Gun.

17 DAVID'S TOWER

Beneath the Half-Moon Battery's gun platform lie the ruins of David's Tower, named after King David II, who commissioned it. This colossal structure, originally standing over 30m high and bristling with 'fish-tailed' arrow slits, took nine years to build. It was not complete when King David died in the castle in 1371. Only part of the ground floor remains, for the tower was brought crashing down during the Lang Siege of 1571–3.

Much of what remains beneath the Half-Moon Battery isn't actually part of David's Tower. The dank cellars were built after 1573 as temporary barracks during siege, 40 men to a cellar. The thick stone vaults above their heads could withstand a direct hit from a mortar bomb. Alas, they couldn't keep out disease, and it was probably here that most of the 70-odd men killed during the 1689 Jacobite siege died, very likely of water poisoning. The casualties also included the lieutenant-governor's cow, wounded by a musket ball.

CROWN SQUARE

Near the entrance to David's Tower, a narrow opening leads into the heart of the castle. Crown Square was created in the late 15th century as the principal courtyard of the castle. The name 'Crown Square' came into use after Sir Walter Scott's discovery of the Scottish Crown and the other royal regalia in the Royal Palace in 1818; before then it was known as Grand Parade, and before that Palace Yard.

Around the four sides of the square were ranged the most important buildings of the castle – the Royal Palace, where the sovereign resided; the Great Hall, the major place of ceremony; the Royal Gunhouse, where Mons Meg and the other great guns were displayed; and St Mary's, the castle church. The last two have long been demolished and replaced. The Queen Anne Building replaced the Royal Gunhouse in the early 18th century; and the Scottish National War Memorial now stands where St Mary's used to be. Yet Crown Square still retains much of its ancient atmosphere of enclosed privilege.

The castle was never a favourite residence of the royal family. Alexander III's first queen, Margaret, pronounced it a 'sad and solitary place, without greenery and, because of its nearness to the sea, unwholesome' – probably a reference to the 'haar', or thick sea-mist, that still envelops the rock from time to time. Only when their safety was threatened did they lodge here.

A stone plaque in the corner of the square, between the Royal Palace and the Great Hall, records the death here on 11 June 1560 of Marie de Guise, James V's widow and Queen-Regnant. This was a time of great national tension that resulted in the Protestant Reformation.

Left: A stylised unicorn, supporter of the Royal Arms of Scotland, guards the entrance to the Scottish National War Memorial.

Opposite: The Royal Palace dominates Crown Square at the heart of the castle.

[18] THE ROYAL PALACE

The Royal Palace was the royal residence in the castle. It began as an extension to David's Tower in the 1430s, and was further enlarged to become the royal residence itself. The last sovereign to sleep here was Charles I on 19 June 1633, the night before his Scottish coronation.

Little remains of the original building, the King's Great Chamber, built for James I in 1434–5. Only the stone-vaulted storage cellars have survived. But the Royal Palace of the later 15th century is still standing. Original features include two fine fireplaces inside on the ground floor and, on the exterior, the stumps of three oriels (projecting windows) on the east elevation overlooking the Old Town. These would have given the royal residents stunning views over the city. The oriels were badly damaged in the bombardment of 1573 that ended the Lang Siege.

The single most important event to take place in the Royal Palace occurred on 19 June 1566 – the birth of James VI of Scotland and I of England. His mother,

Above (left): The cramped birthchamber where Mary Queen of Scots gave birth to her only child, James VI.

Above (right): A portrait of James VI, painted around 1620. His last visit to his birthplace was in 1617.

Below: A gilded stone panel shows 1566, the date of James's birth, and the interlocking initials 'MAH', for his parents Mary and Henry.

Mary Queen of Scots, had taken up residence in April 1566, moving up from Holyrood Palace with her furniture and furnishings, including her great four-poster bed hung with blue velvet and taffeta. Shortly after the birth, which took place between 10 and 11 in the morning, Mary had Prince James taken from his cradle, wrapped in the finest robes, and presented to her closest courtiers. These included the baby's father, Henry Lord Darnley, though in truth Mary and Darnley were by now estranged.

Nothing of the majesty of Queen Mary's apartment survives, but above the round-headed doorway leading from Crown Square to the 'Mary Room' is a gilded panel bearing the date 1566 and the entwined initials MAH, for Mary and Henry, James's parents.

James VI returned to his birthplace in 1617, as part of his Golden Jubilee celebrations. The royal visit prompted a complete remodelling of the Royal Palace inside and out, and many of the features you can now see date from then. They include, on the outside, the dates 1615 and 1616, the cannon-studded battlemented parapet, the square turrets with their ogee-shaped roofs, and ornate window pediments carved with royal emblems – the Crown, the Scottish thistle, the English rose, the French fleur-de-lis, the Irish harp and the monogram IR6 (for Iacobus Rex 6). Two large panels on the east elevation displayed the Honours of Scotland and the Royal Arms of Scotland; the latter was defaced during Cromwell's occupation in the 1650s.

Internally, new state rooms were created. These included the Laich (or lower) Hall on the ground floor – which has recently been recreated – as well as private apartments for the king and queen and lodgings for court officials. The ceiling of the king's birthchamber was specially decorated for his visit. On the first floor, the Crown Room was built as a strongroom to house the Honours of Scotland.

Left: A stone panel marks the date of alterations to the palace made in anticipation of James's 50th anniversary as King of Scots.

Below: A gilded carving shows the Scottish thistle, the Crown and the monogram IR6 – Iacobus Rex 6 – for King James VI.

19 THE HONOURS OF SCOTLAND

The Honours of Scotland – the Crown, Sceptre and Sword of State – are the oldest crown jewels in the British Isles. They were shaped in Scotland and Italy during the reigns of James IV and James V, and first used together for the coronation of Mary Queen of Scots in 1543.

The Honours have had an eventful history. From 1651 to 1660 they lay buried to preserve them from the clutches of Oliver Cromwell, first at Dunnottar Castle, near Stonehaven, and then under the floor of nearby Kinneff Church. After the 1707 Treaty of Union they were locked away in the Crown Room. In 1818 Walter Scott, with royal approval, had the room broken into and the oak chest in which they had been kept forced open. He found them as they had been left 111 years earlier.

The **Sword of State**, created along with its scabbard and belt by the Italian cutler Domenico da Sutri, was presented to James IV by Pope Julius II in 1507. The fracture in the sword's blade was probably made prior to smuggling the Honours out of Dunnottar in 1652.

Opposite: The Crown, made in its present form in 1540.

Opposite (far right): The Sceptre, presented to James IV by Pope Alexander VI in 1494, then lengthened in 1536.

Below: The Sword of State, presented to James IV by Pope Julius II in 1507.

DID YOU KNOW...

A fourth object, a silver-gilt wand, was found in the oak chest alongside the Honours of Scotland in 1818. No one knows why it was there, but it too is on display in the Crown Room.

'The extreme solemnity of opening sealed doors of oak and iron, and finally breaking open a chest which had been shut since 7th March 1707, about a hundred and eleven years, gave a sort of interest to our researches, which I can hardly express to you, and it would be very difficult to describe the intense eagerness with which we watched the rising of the lid of the chest.'

Sir Walter Scott, in a letter to John Wilson Croker, 7 February 1818.

The **Crown** was made for James V in 1540 by John Mosman, an Edinburgh goldsmith. Mosman melted down the gold from the old crown, added more Scottish gold to it, and studded the new circlet with gemstones. The king first wore his new Crown at the coronation of Queen Marie de Guise in Holyrood Abbey in 1540.

The **Sceptre** was presented to James IV, probably in 1494 by Pope Alexander VI. James V had it lengthened in 1536 by the Edinburgh silversmith, Andrew Leys. The upper part of the rod, decorated with Scottish thistles, is Leys's work.

Above: The Ruby Ring, bequeathed to George III in 1807 by Cardinal Henry York, brother of Bonnie Prince Charlie.

Above: The gold and enamel Collar of the Order of the Garter, also bequeathed by Cardinal York in 1807.

Above: The padlock from the chest that contained the Honours of Scotland. It was broken when they were rediscovered in 1818.

THE STONE OF DESTINY

On 30 November 1996, St Andrew's Day, Edinburgh Castle became the home of another Scottish icon – the Stone of Destiny.

For centuries, the Stone of Destiny served as the seat on which the Scottish kings were enthroned at Scone, near Perth. Then, in 1296, Edward I of England, 'Hammer of the Scots', had it forcibly removed. When it arrived in Westminster Abbey in London it was enclosed within a new throne, the Coronation Chair. Since then, the Stone has been used in the coronation ceremonies of most of the monarchs of England, and from 1714 all the sovereigns of Great Britain (apart from Edward VIII, who was never crowned).

Now the ancient Stone rests again in Scotland, in the Crown Room beside the Honours of Scotland. It will only ever leave Scotland again when there is a coronation in Westminster Abbey.

DID YOU KNOW ...

On Christmas Day 1950 four Scottish students removed the Stone of Destiny from Westminster Abbey. Three months later it turned up 500 miles away – at the front door of Arbroath Abbey.

20 THE GREAT HALL

The Great Hall was completed in 1511, and was intended to serve as the chief place of ceremony in the castle. Sadly it saw little of that. James IV, who commissioned it, was killed at the Battle of Flodden two years later, and his heirs much preferred the salubrious surroundings of Holyrood to the imposing heights of Castle Rock. When Cromwell captured the castle in 1650 he had the enormous space converted into barracks to accommodate his troops, and it remained in military use for the next 230 years.

When the army vacated the building in 1886, work began to restore it to its former glory. The Edinburgh architect, Hippolyte Blanc, orchestrated almost everything you see inside – the impressive hooded fireplace, the heavy Gothic timber entrance screen and panelling, the heraldic stained glass, the lighting and flooring. The only exception is the great hammerbeam roof high above your head.

Above: A detail from the hooded fireplace.

Left: An 18th-century halberd, one of the many weapons on display in the Great Hall, which are on loan from the Royal Armouries.

DID YOU KNOW...

The iron-barred opening above and to the right of the great fireplace was a peephole (called a 'laird's lug' in Scotland), from where the king could spy or eavesdrop on his courtiers. The KGB asked that it be bricked up prior to Mikhael Gorbachev's planned visit in 1984.

This medieval roof is one of the most important in Britain. The stone corbels supporting the main trusses are carved with Renaissance sculpture, the oldest surviving in Britain, pre-dating by a decade Benedetto da Maiano's roundels at Hampton Court in London. Features to look out for include the cipher IR4 – 'Iacobus Rex 4' – for James IV; the crowned Royal Arms; Scottish thistles; fleurs-de-lis symbolising the 'Auld Alliance' with France; and vases containing both thistles and roses, symbolising the new English connection brought about when James IV married Margaret Tudor in 1503.

Above (main image): The Great Hall was built in the early 16th century, though it was extensively refurbished in the 1880s.

Above (details): The stone corbels are decorated with Renaissance sculptures:

1 Christian symbol. IHS stands for *Jesus Hominum Salvator*: 'Jesus, Saviour to men'.

2 A woman with red roses, possibly representing Venus.

3 The Green Man, a pre-Christian symbol of fertility.

4 A pair of thistles, the plant badge of Scotland.

5 The fleur-de-lis, representing both France and the Virgin Mary.

6 The Royal Arms of James IV.

7 A vase containing Scottish thistles and an English rose.

8 The crowned Royal Arms of Scotland.

21 THE SCOTTISH NATIONAL WAR MEMORIAL

In the Middle Ages, the castle church of St Mary graced the north side of Crown Square. Following James V's development of Holyrood Palace in the 1530s, the church was converted into a munitions store. It was eventually demolished in 1754 and replaced by the North Barracks.

When the garrison left the castle in 1923, the opportunity was taken to adapt the barracks as the Scottish National War Memorial to the dead of the First World War. The architect was Sir Robert Lorimer, and the cream of Scottish artists and craftsmen and women took part in its creation. The Duke of Rothesay (the future Edward VIII) formally opened Scotland's National Shrine on 14 July 1927, in the presence of Their Majesties King George V and Queen Mary. The building now also commemorates those who fell in the Second World War and in military campaigns since 1945.

The exterior of the Memorial is enriched with sculpture symbolising the 'Just War'. The animals in the windows and niches represent the Vices and Virtues. The human figures on the Crown Square elevation signify, from left to right, Courage (a figure wearing chain mail with sword and shield), Peace (a female figure with doves), Mercy (a warrior with a child) and Justice (blindfolded with scales and a sword). The figure above the entrance, shown rising from a phoenix, represents the survival of the Spirit.

Inside is the Hall of Honour, originally called the Hall of the Regiments. Here the enormous contribution of Scotland's 12 regiments and the other corps and services are recorded. Beyond lies the Shrine, where the Rolls of Honour of the Scottish dead of the Great War are kept in a steel casket. The figure of St Michael the Archangel soars overhead. The stained-glass windows and bronze friezes give vivid impressions of the First World War.

Above (top): The Scottish National War Memorial was created in 1923, adapted from an abandoned barracks.

Above (middle): The stained glass depicts vivid scenes from the First World War.

Left: Scenes from the First World War are also modelled in bronze around the walls of the Shrine.

Opposite: The Shrine, overseen by St Michael the Archangel.

THE QUEEN ANNE BUILDING

The Queen Anne Building stands opposite the Royal Palace, in a position once occupied by the Royal Gunhouse, where Mons Meg was kept. By 1700 it had gone, and the present building was constructed following the failed Jacobite Rising of 1708, to provide rooms for staff officers and the castle gunners.

The building was vacated in 1923 and reopened in 1933 as the Scottish Naval and Military Museum, to complement the Scottish National War Memorial adjacent. That museum has since become the National War Museum and is now sited elsewhere in the castle (see page 12). The Queen Anne Building now houses a café and function suite, as well as the castle's education centre.

Below (top left):
The vaults beneath Crown Square are bleak spaces that were used as prisons for centuries.

Below (bottom left):
Graffiti carved in stone by a French prisoner.

Below (main image):
The cells have been reconstructed to show how they would have looked in the late 18th century.

22 PRISONS OF WAR

Deep beneath the Great Hall and Queen Anne Building are two tiers of cavernous stone vaults. Over the centuries they have been put to all sorts of use – stores for food and military supplies, soldiers' barracks, a bakery, state and military prisons.

But their use as prisons of war captures our imagination most. The first prisoners of war, the French crew of a privateer captured in the North Sea, arrived in 1758, soon after the outbreak of the Seven Years War with France. By the end of the war in 1763 they had been joined by 500 more.

The vaults were used as prisons again during the War of American Independence (1775–83). Once again almost all the POWs were sailors, but this time they included not only Frenchmen, but also Spaniards, Dutchmen, Irishmen – and of course Americans. Some of those 'damned Yankees' were in fact Scots who had emigrated to North America and become caught up in that momentous conflict. They included two sailors from the fleet of Captain John Paul Jones, 'the father of the American Navy' who was himself a Scot.

The vaults' role as prisons came to a peak during the wars with Revolutionary and Napoleonic France (1793–1815). Again, most of the POWs were sailors, including a five-year-old drummer boy taken at Trafalgar, but soldiers later arrived from Spain and Portugal, where Sir Arthur Wellesley (later the Duke of Wellington) won some important victories over Napoleonic forces. The prisoners came from many different backgrounds, and in the crowded, squalid conditions feuds developed between the various nationalities.

Escape was never far from their minds. One prisoner hid in a dung barrow, only to be dashed to pieces on the rocks below when the contents were tipped over the castle wall. Four more escaped in 1799 by lowering themselves down the rock on their washing lines. The most audacious breakout occurred in 1811, when 49 prisoners cut their way through the parapet wall beside the battery; all but one escaped. The hole is still there.

Above: Removal of paint from a door in the vaults revealed that one room was used to store hospital bedding, probably around 1810.

Above (top left): A scale model of the HMS *St George*, built by French prisoners in 1760 for the Duke of Atholl.

DID YOU KNOW...

Twenty-one pirates from the Caribbean were imprisoned in the vaults in 1720. They had been captured off the Argyll coast and brought to the castle pending their trial. It was claimed that their ship's hold was full of Portuguese and French gold. Most were found guilty of piracy and hanged below the High Water Mark off Leith.

23 DURY'S BATTERY

The POWs spent most of their waking day out in their exercise yard on Dury's Battery, named after Captain Theodore Dury, the military engineer who designed it and the Queen Anne Building after the 1708 Jacobite Rising. There they sold objects made out of old bones, bits of wood and bedstraw to the Edinburgh townsfolk through the yard's perimeter fence. Scale models of ships and intricate little workboxes were the most popular purchases; the more resourceful POWs forged banknotes!

Bottom: Dury's Battery is well defended and offered prisoners of war little chance of escape.

Below: A key used in the Military Prison, where unruly soldiers of the garrison were locked up.

24 MILITARY PRISON

The Military Prison was built in 1842 for defaulting soldiers from the garrison, for offences such as 'drunk on guard'. In the 1880s it was extended, increasing the number of cells from 12 to 16, providing separate ablution blocks, and rooms for the provost marshal, the officer in charge. The prison was a miniature version of the great civilian prisons of the day, such as Barlinnie in Glasgow. The prisoners were held in solitary confinement, and compelled to do four hours of hard punishment a day – such as working a treadmill, a machine not unlike an exercise bike.

BUTTS BATTERY AND BACK WELL

Behind the Governor's House is a cluster of buildings dating mostly from the 18th century. This area provided rough grazing throughout the Middle Ages, and the name of the gun battery at the rear, Butts Battery, gives a clue to the role the area played during the Wars of Independence – as a place where the garrison perfected their archery skills at the target, or 'butts'.

The ground was only developed after 1600 to accommodate the fast-expanding garrison. Long-demolished 17th-century buildings included barracks, a malt barn and a firework laboratory. Only one structure survives from that century – the Back Well, dug in 1628. A mere 2.5m deep, it was more a cistern than a well, collecting the water that drained through fissures in the rock.

Opposite: The main staircase and cells of the Military Prison. The prison was expanded in the 1880s, in response to new health regulations.

25 THE WESTERN DEFENCES

Defensive walls have enclosed the precipitous west side of the castle since at least the 17th century. To visit the this part of the castle, you must follow the cobbled road back down the hill to the Redcoat Café. To the right of the Cartshed building you will find access to the Western Defences via the One o'Clock Gun exhibition.

However, please note that the Western Defences are sometimes closed to visitors, especially when the weather is bad. The hazards of patrolling here were made clear in a 1677 report observing that sentries found them impossible to 'go along in a stormy night'.

Halfway along the Western Defences, there is a small back gate known as the Sallyport. On the night of 19 March 1689, Viscount Dundee, leader of the Jacobite faction in Parliament, met secretly here with the castle governor, the Duke of Gordon, also a Jacobite. After their meeting, Dundee rode north to raise an army to fight for the exiled James VII, while Gordon continued to hold the castle for the Jacobites.

Even though the garrison numbered barely 120 men, and there were just 100 barrels of powder for the 22 guns, they held out for three months. When Gordon eventually surrendered, just 50 emaciated soldiers remained alive.

Below: The formidable Western Defences, as seen from the Ross Fountain in West Princes Street Gardens.

During the 1715 Rising, the Jacobites almost succeeded in breaching these defences, prompting a fundamental redesign. The Sallyport was blocked up, new sentry boxes were built at the angles of the defensive wall (one intriguingly called the Queen's Post) and a new guardhouse (demolished around 1850) was built for the patrols.

DID YOU KNOW...

In the 1850s a grandiose scheme was launched to transform this side of the castle into a 'fairytale château'. Work even began. The terrace above the grassy bank of the Western Defences has the date 1858 carved on it, and the stumps of masonry you can now see projecting from it were intended to form part of a fanciful turret. Mercifully, common sense prevailed and the foolhardy project was killed off.

LEAVING THE CASTLE

As you make your way out of the castle, you will pass through a series of gateways belonging to different periods in its history.

THE PORTCULLIS GATE

This 16th-century fortification is where our tour began. As you leave, notice the decorations just outside the archway. The stone panel above the outer gate is decorated with hearts and stars, the armorial insignia of James Douglas, Earl of Morton. As Regent of Scotland for the young James VI, he commissioned the Portcullis Gate. The shield displaying the Lion Rampant, the Scottish Royal Arms, was inserted in 1887, when the decorative upper story, the Argyle Tower, was added.

A plaque high up on the wall on your right records the exploits of Sir William Kirkcaldy of Grange, who commanded the castle during the Lang Siege.

THE INNER BARRIER

The next gateway you will pass through is the 17th-century Inner Barrier. Now reduced to a pair of stone gateposts and a sturdy, sloping wall, it was originally much more formidable, with a drawbridge and ditch in front of it. The Old Guardhouse on your left, now a gift shop, began as a gun platform protecting that barrier. When the latter became redundant around 1850, the platform was roofed over and converted into a guardhouse and prison.

THE GATEHOUSE

The Gatehouse was built in 1888 with the sole intention of making the castle look more imposing. It replaced a much simpler 17th-century gate. Inside the archway, high up on the side walls, are two 17th-century stone panels depicting Mons Meg and other munitions then kept in the castle.

Outside, set into the façade, are bronze statues of King Robert the Bruce on the left and Sir William Wallace on the right. These were added in 1929, to mark the 600th anniversary of Bruce's death. However there is no record that either patriot ever visited the castle.

THE ESPLANADE

The Esplanade was formed in 1753 as a parade ground for the castle garrison, and has been used for military spectacles ever since. Each August since 1950 it has hosted performances of the world-famous Edinburgh Military Tattoo.

Prior to 1753, though, the Esplanade was a rugged open landscape where the citizens came to watch far more grisly spectacles. Castle Hill was a place of execution, where women accused of witchcraft, religious dissenters and others who had fallen foul of the sovereign were hanged or burned at the stake.

Above: One of two 17th-century stone carvings inside the Gatehouse arch, featuring Mons Meg and other weaponry held in the castle.

Left: Part of the Esplanade and the Gatehouse, which was added in 1888 to provide the castle with an imposing new entrance.

Opposite (far left): The bronze statue of William Wallace was added in 1929, along with a similar representation of Robert the Bruce.

DID YOU KNOW...

In 1989, archaeologists unearthed 15 skeletons in the area where the new ticket facility now stands. The bones belonged to soldiers who had died defending the castle during the first Jacobite Rising of 1689. Their bodies could not be taken for burial in the town because the castle was under siege.

THE STORY OF
EDINBURGH CASTLE

EDINBURGH CASTLE – SYMBOL OF SCOTLAND

Three thousand years of history are hidden away in the mighty royal castle of Edinburgh. In that time, the Castle Rock has been visited by Roman legionaries, Anglian warlords, Saxon princesses, Norman knights, English invaders, Caribbean pirates and prisoners of war from France, Spain, the Netherlands and America. The castle's colourful story is told in the following pages.

'...so strongly grounded, bounded and founded that by force of man it can never be confounded'

John Taylor, *The Penniless Pilgrimage*, 1618.

Left: A painting of the castle from the Grassmarket, around 1790, by the Edinburgh artist Alexander Nasmyth.

Above: The Lion Rampant within its double tressure has been the emblem of Scotland for 800 years.

DIN EIDYN

The Castle Rock was created 340 million years ago during a period of volcanic activity. Molten magma from deep in the earth erupted into the atmosphere. For hundreds, perhaps thousands of years, lava oozed forth, creating a huge volcano. Eventually the lava cooled. Millions of years passed. The volcano became buried beneath sedimentary rocks.

When the Ice Ages came, the ice sheets peeled away those sedimentary rocks. The last Ice Age, which ended over 10,000 years ago, left little behind but the core of the volcano. The hard volcanic rock protected the sedimentary rocks to its east, and by the time the ice had melted away, the world's best-known 'crag-and-tail' – now the Castle Rock and Royal Mile – had been formed.

Our earliest evidence for human settlement on the rock comes in the Bronze Age, about 900 BC. Archaeological excavations convey a picture of clusters of large round-houses spread over the rock. It was quite a bustling hillfort by the time Roman legionaries arrived, around AD 78.

Below: Two Roman bronze brooches, around 2,000 years old, were found at the castle.

DID YOU KNOW…

In the early 19th century, a 7th-century Pictish stone, carved with a crescent and V-shaped rod and double-disc with Z-shaped rod, was found during the creation of Princes Street Gardens. This suggests that the people from north of the Forth settled in Edinburgh for a time.

The Romans called the local tribe the Votadini. In time they became known as the Gododdin (pronounced *god-oth-in*). And it is with them that the Castle Rock first appears in the historical record around AD 600 – as *Din Eidyn,* 'the stronghold of Eidyn'. Who or what Eidyn was remains a mystery, though legend tells of a giant called the Red Etin. But the rock by now was the stronghold of their king, Mynyddog 'the Magnificent'.

Y Gododdin, a poem by Mynyddog's bard, Aneirin, records a great battle in Yorkshire between the Gododdin and the Angles, recent invaders from Europe, who gave England its name. It proved disastrous for the Gododdin, and Din Eidyn was captured in 638. The Angles renamed the rock Edinburgh, the English name it has kept ever since.

Left: An artist's impression of the Gododdin leaving Din Eidyn for their catastrophic battle with the Angles.

Opposite (main image): A view of the castle from the nearby volcanic outcrop of the Salisbury Crags.

'The Castle dominated
the Edinburgh skyline…
Its volcanic sides seemed
sheer and impregnable –
and so they had proved
down the years.'

Ian Rankin, *The Naming of the Dead.*

TIMELINE

c.900 BC

EARLIEST EVIDENCE
of humans living on
the Castle Rock.

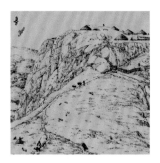

c.AD 600

DIN EIDYN
appears for the first
time in historical
records as the name
of the stronghold.

THE 'CASTLE OF MAIDENS'

Around 843, the Picts and Scots living north of the Forth and Clyde united to become one nation – Scotland. Soon they were making inroads into Anglian territory. In 1018, Malcolm II of Scotland defeated the Angles, or English as they were now called, at Carham on the River Tweed, 50 miles (80km) south of Edinburgh. Edinburgh was free from English rule at last.

Below left: King Malcolm III and Queen Margaret – later St Margaret – as depicted in the *Seton Armorial*.

Opposite: The Royal Mile, with the castle at the top.

In 1093 we read of a royal castle on the rock, known as the 'Castle of Maidens'. Why 'Maidens' is unclear, though there was a story that the Picts used to keep virgins here. In November that year Queen Margaret was in residence. Her husband, Malcolm Canmore (Malcolm III), was away fighting in Northumberland. Then disaster struck. Malcolm was killed near Alnwick, along with his eldest son. On hearing the news, Margaret took to her bed and died.

In the reign of David I (1142–53), Edinburgh Castle became a major royal fortress. Responsibility for keeping it well defended fell to the king's constable, or keeper. Over the centuries, the constable came to be known as the governor.

DID YOU KNOW...

In 1989, archaeologists digging at Mills Mount discovered an ancient cobbled track leading west out of the castle. This may just have been the route along which Queen Margaret's coffin was taken when her body was smuggled out of the castle in November 1093.

1093

QUEEN MARGARET of Scotland, Malcolm Canmore's widow, dies in the castle. She is canonised as Saint Margaret in 1251.

c.1130

ST MARGARET'S CHAPEL is built by her son, David I, at Edinburgh Castle, where it still stands.

This early castle was mainly confined to the rock's summit, and would have been built largely of timber. Only tiny St Margaret's Chapel and the larger St Mary's Church (on the site where the Scottish National War Memorial now stands), are known to have been built of stone. It is likely that most of the buildings and defences were rebuilt in stone in the 13th century.

But the stone walls were still not strong enough to withstand the armed might of the English following Edward I's invasion in early 1296. Their capture of the fortress heralded a new era for the royal castle.

KINGS AND QUEENS OF SCOTLAND PART 1: CANMORE DYNASTY

Malcolm III (1058–93)
1093: Killed fighting the Normans in Northumberland. 1093: Queen Margaret (later St Margaret of Scotland) dies in castle on hearing of her husband's death.

Donald III (1093–4)
1093: Queen Margaret's body smuggled out of castle and buried in Dunfermline Abbey.

Duncan II (1094)

Donald III (1094–97)

Edgar (1097–1107)
1107: Dies in Edinburgh Castle.

Alexander I (1107–24)

David I (1124–53)
1128: Founds Holyrood Abbey in Edinburgh. c. 1130: Builds St Margaret's Chapel, in honour of his mother, within Edinburgh Castle.

Malcolm IV (1153–65)

William I (1165–1214)
1174: Captured in Northumberland fighting the English. 1174–1186: Edinburgh Castle held by English.

Alexander II (1214–49)

Alexander III (1249–86)
1263: Defeats King Hakon of Norway at Largs, effectively bringing the Hebrides back under Scottish rule. 1278: His queen, Margaret, describes castle as 'this sad and solitary place'.

Margaret (1286–90)
1290: Dies without ever setting foot in Scotland.

Interregnum (1290–92)
1290–1: Edward I of England presides over 'the Great Cause' to determine who should rule Scotland. 1291: Edward I stays in castle.

WAR WITH ENGLAND

I t was only after three days of artillery bombardment that the English captured Edinburgh Castle in 1296. They held it for the next 18 years.

It had to be won back. But how? In the end it took a great feat of daring by Robert the Bruce's nephew, Sir Thomas Randolph, Earl of Moray.

The assault took place on the evening of 14 March 1314, and the weather was foul. While the English guards were distracted by a disturbance at the main gate, Randolph's assault party made their perilous ascent up the northern precipice, scaled the castle wall and caught the enemy completely off guard.

Following the castle's recapture, it was dismantled by the Scots on Bruce's orders, to make it unusable by the English. Three months later, Bruce won his great victory over the English at Bannockburn.

The great fortress lay in ruins for the next 20 years. But on Bruce's death in 1329, war broke out again and by 1335 the castle was back in English hands. And once more it took a feat of bravery and cunning to win the castle back.

Left: The bronze statue of Robert the Bruce, at the main entrance to the castle.

Below: The castle at sunset.

This time Sir William Douglas spearheaded the assault. In April 1341, a ship supposedly carrying provisions for the beleaguered English garrison arrived at Leith. On board were 200 Scots masquerading as sailors. The following day they made their way up to the castle with their consignment. The garrison, suspecting nothing, lowered the drawbridge to let them in. But as the party passed through, they dropped their casks and sacks to prevent the gates closing and overcame the startled guards.

Douglas and his followers rushed from their hiding place nearby and helped overwhelm the rest of the garrison – over 100 men, including 60 archers. They were shown no mercy; their throats were cut and their corpses thrown over the crags.

Shortly afterwards, David II, Bruce's son, returned to Scotland to begin his own reign. He rebuilt the castle, adding David's Tower, which is named after him. He died in the castle in February 1371.

KINGS AND QUEENS OF SCOTLAND PART II: BALLIOL AND BRUCE

John (1292–6)

Interregnum (1296–1306)
1296: Edward I captures Edinburgh Castle after the Battle of Dunbar.

1296: Stone of Destiny removed by Edward I from Scone, Perthshire, to Westminster Abbey.

Robert I 'the Bruce' (1306–29)
1314: Recaptures Edinburgh Castle and orders its destruction.

1314: Defeats Edward II of England at the Battle of Bannockburn.

David II (1329–71)
1346: Captured by English near Durham and imprisoned in Tower of London for 10 years.

1371: Dies in Edinburgh Castle without seeing his new royal residence, David's Tower, finished.

'Then the English garrison vented their fury overmuch on the poor common people.'

Abbot Walter Bower, *Chronicle of the Scots,* 15th century, describing an action in the winter of 1337–8 after an attempt by the Scots to recapture Edinburgh Castle.

Above: The Stone of Destiny was taken to Westminster by Edward I in 1296.

1296	1314	1341

EDWARD I of England captures castle after a three-day bombardment.

ROBERT THE BRUCE'S army recaptures the castle after a daring night-time attack. It falls to the English again in 1335.

A SCOTTISH RAID led by Sir William Douglas recaptures the castle once again.

KINGS AND QUEENS OF SCOTLAND PART III: STEWART DYNASTY

Robert II (1371–90)

Robert III (1390–1406)
1398: Holds jousting tournament in Edinburgh.

James I (1406–37)
1434: Builds the Great Chamber (now Laich Hall). 1437: Killed by his own nobles in Perth.

James II (1437–60)
1440: Aged nine, hosts the infamous 'Black Dinner'. 1460: Killed when one of his own guns explodes at siege of Roxburgh Castle.

James III (1460–88)
1482: Held prisoner inside Edinburgh Castle. 1488: Murdered after the Battle of Sauchieburn.

James IV (1488–1513)
1507: Receives Sword of State from Pope Julius II. 1513: Killed at the Battle of Flodden.

James V (1513–42)
1540: Has the Crown remade to its present form. 1542: Dies following the Battle of Solway Moss.

Mary I ('Queen of Scots') (1542–67)
1566: Gives birth in Edinburgh Castle to James, the future king of both Scotland and England. 1567: Forced to abdicate in favour of her son.

James VI (1567–1625)
1603: Becomes King James I of England following death of Queen Elizabeth. 1617: Has the Royal Palace in Edinburgh Castle refurbished.

Charles I (1625–49)
1633: Becomes the last sovereign to sleep in Edinburgh Castle. 1649: Executed in London on the orders of Oliver Cromwell.

Charles II (1649–85)
1650: Cromwell invades Scotland and seizes Edinburgh Castle. 1651: Charles crowned King of Scots at Scone, with the Honours of Scotland.

James VII (1685–89)
1689: Overthrown by William and Mary and forced into permanent exile.

Mary II (1689–94)

William II (1689–1702)
1689: The Duke of Gordon surrenders Edinburgh Castle after a three-month siege.

Anne (1702–14)
1707: Honours of Scotland hidden in the Crown Room following Treaty of Union with England.

A ROYAL CASTLE

David II's death brought the Bruce dynasty to a close, and ushered in the age of the Royal Stewarts. During their time, Edinburgh Castle reached the pinnacle of its importance as Scotland's principal royal castle.

The emergence of Edinburgh as the nation's capital during James III's reign was chiefly responsible. He made the castle his permanent home, replanning the royal residence around a new central courtyard, Crown Square. The rebuilding reached its stunning climax during the reign of his son James IV, with the completion of the Great Hall in 1511.

By now the castle was serving not only as a royal residence but also as the repository of the Honours, the state archives and the royal artillery, including Mons Meg. It provided residences for high-ranking officials as well as prison accommodation.

The state jail wasn't entirely escape-proof, as the Duke of Albany, James III's brother, proved in 1479. After killing his guards, Albany lowered himself down the rock on a rope tied to the bars of his prison window and fled to France.

But the castle, perched high on its rock, was never a comfortable residence. Bishop Douglas of Dunkeld summed up its chief drawbacks – 'windy and richt unpleasand'. And so the Royal Stewarts decided that Holyrood Abbey, down at the far end of the Royal Mile, was more to their liking. By the time of the Protestant Reformation in 1560, the ancient abbey had become the new Palace of Holyrood. Draughty Edinburgh Castle would henceforth be used only when the royal family's security was threatened, or when protocol demanded.

Both factors combined in 1566 when Mary Queen of Scots became pregnant, for her child would be heir to two thrones: not only the Scottish one, but also the English. Mary took up residence in the castle in April, and on the morning of Wednesday 19 June she gave birth to Prince James, who would one day rule as James VI of Scotland and I of England.

Above: A painting of the castle around 1780 by the Edinburgh artist Alexander Nasmyth. This view from what is now Waverley station shows the Nor' Loch, now drained to form Princes Street Gardens.

Opposite: Mary Queen of Scots, probably painted during the 1560s.

DID YOU KNOW...

In 1830, during building works in the Royal Palace, the remains of a child's body were discovered, wrapped in a white cloth on which the letter 'J' could be made out. The items were subsequently lost, but the rumour spread that the body was that of a stillborn baby supposedly born to Mary Queen of Scots in 1566.

1457

1566

MONS MEG arrives in Edinburgh, a gift to James II from his wife's uncle Duke Philip of Burgundy.

JAMES VI IS BORN in the castle. He succeeds his mother Mary Queen of Scots the following year and in 1603 becomes James I of England.

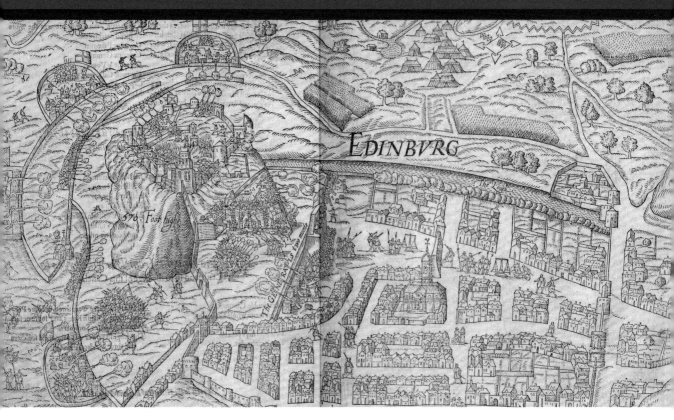

> 'No mining can prevail
> in this rock but only
> battery with ordnance
> to beat down the walls.'

An English spy's assessment of the
castle's strength, April 1544.

Edinburgh Castel

THE 'LANG SIEGE' OF 1571-3

On 6 May 1567, Mary Queen of Scots entered the castle for the last time. The guns 'schot maist magnificentlie' to welcome her and her lover, the Earl of Bothwell. Nine days later they were married. The union proved disastrous and provoked Mary's nobles to rebel. She was soon caught and imprisoned in Lochleven Castle, near Kinross, where she was compelled to abdicate in favour of her son, James VI. Ten months later she escaped, but after a valiant rearguard action she was forced to flee to the safety, so she thought, of her cousin, Queen Elizabeth of England.

1567

1573

MARY QUEEN OF SCOTS
visits the castle for the third
and final time.

SIR WILLIAM KIRKCALDY
of Grange is forced to
surrender the castle,
bringing an end to
the Lang Siege.

Despite her departure, some people in Scotland continued to support Mary's cause – among them Sir William Kirkcaldy of Grange, governor of Edinburgh Castle. By the summer of 1571 he was defiantly holding the fortress against the regent governing on behalf of the infant James. The siege dragged on for well over a year and became known as the Lang (long) Siege.

In desperation, the besiegers turned to Queen Elizabeth for help. She lent them 20 heavy guns, and a few days after the bombardment began, much of the east side of the castle was brought crashing down, including David's Tower. With the Fore Well choked with rubble, thereby cutting off the water supply, Kirkcaldy surrendered.

Most of the beleaguered garrison were allowed to go free, but not Sir William. The great soldier was ignominiously hauled behind a cart through the streets of Edinburgh to the mercat cross in the Royal Mile and executed. His severed head was impaled on a spike on the castle walls he had so resolutely defended.

Following the siege, David's Tower was abandoned and the Half-Moon Battery was built around its ruins. The Portcullis Gate was also built to replace the Constable's Tower as the castle's main entrance. The badly damaged Royal Palace lay unused by royalty for 42 years, until James VI ordered its reconstruction, prior to his 'hamecoming' in 1617 to celebrate his 50th anniversary as King of Scots.

DID YOU KNOW…

In 1997, during restoration of the Royal Palace, a medieval latrine closet was found in a wall of the Laich Hall. It had been blocked up in 1615 with stones from the oriel windows that had once graced the east face of the building, until its destruction in the Lang Siege.

Opposite (main image): An illustration from Raphael Holinshed's famous *Chronicles of England, Scotland and Ireland,* showing the Lang Siege. The book was published soon after the event, in 1577.

Opposite (below left): An English spy's drawing of the castle, made in 1544, shows David's Tower still standing.

Left: Soon after the destruction of David's Tower in 1573, the Half-Moon Battery was built around its ruins.

'There are armed men and cannon in the citadel overhead; you may see the troops marshalled on the high parade; and at night after the early winter evenfall, and in the morning before the laggard winter dawn, the wind carries abroad over Edinburgh the sound of drums and bugles.'

Robert Louis Stevenson, *Edinburgh, Picturesque Notes*, 1878.

DID YOU KNOW...

Popular belief has it that the Esplanade is actually Canadian soil. The misconception dates from the 1620s, when James VI supported a scheme to colonise Nova Scotia. But aspiring baronets were saved the daunting journey to their new estate. All they had to do to claim their title was trek to the Castle Hill, in Edinburgh, and receive a handful of earth, symbolising Nova Scotian soil.

GARRISON FORTRESS

In 1633, Charles I slept in the castle the night before his Scottish coronation. He was the last reigning sovereign to stay here. Charles's execution in 1649, and the unequivocal support of the Scots for his rightful successor, Charles II, brought Oliver Cromwell to Scotland. By Christmas Day 1650, the Lord Protector of England had captured the castle.

The castle now began to take on the appearance of a garrison fortress. Before Cromwell's time, Scotland's common army, the 'host', had been called out only when the need arose, and the castle was 'stuffed with men' only in times of crisis. From now on, the castle would have a permanent garrison.

Much of what visitors see today was built for the army from the 17th century onwards. Some important medieval buildings were demolished, including the Royal Gunhouse, Mons Meg's old lair, removed in 1708 to make way for the Queen Anne Building, and St Mary's Church, replaced in 1755 by the new North Barracks, which now forms the core of the Scottish National War Memorial.

Other structures were converted for army use, including the ancient Royal Palace. Almost every inch of space in this building had a military role, including James VI's birthchamber, which became a small-arms store. The only room not affected was the Crown Room, which was sealed up in 1707 following the Treaty of Union between Scotland and England.

The defences were also rebuilt, for the castle was still a key military target. That became all too clear during the Jacobite Risings that came after James VII's flight into exile in 1689.

Above: One of the cannon ports on the Forewall Battery, with the Scott Monument in the line of fire.

Opposite (main image): A painting from 1860–1 shows the 78th Highlanders stationed at the castle.

1633

1650

CHARLES I
stays in the castle, the
last sovereign to do so.

OLIVER CROMWELL
captures the castle
following his victory at
the Battle of Dunbar.

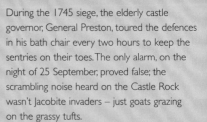

'Orillon where ye Rebels attempted to
surprise ye Castle in ye year 1715.'

A hand-written comment on a 1725 plan of Edinburgh Castle.
An 'orillon' was a defensive structure protecting the Sallyport,
and 'ye Rebels' were the Jacobites.

DID YOU KNOW…

During the 1745 siege, the elderly castle
governor, General Preston, toured the defences
in his bath chair every two hours to keep the
sentries on their toes. The only alarm, on the
night of 25 September, proved false; the
scrambling noise heard on the Castle Rock
wasn't Jacobite invaders – just goats grazing
on the grassy tufts.

JACOBITES AND HANOVERIANS

The Jacobites soon lost control of their departed
sovereign's castle. Despite a determined
resistance in early 1689, the loss of over 70
men compelled the governor, the Duke of Gordon, to
surrender to the incoming sovereigns, William and Mary.

An attempted Jacobite Rising by the exiled James VII
in 1708 failed even before it had begun, but in 1715,
with the accession of George I, Elector of Hanover, to
the British throne, the Jacobites almost succeeded in
retaking the castle.

Above (main image): A painting of the
castle around 1746, which now hangs in the
Prisons of War exhibition.

Their plan was to scale the precipitous rock face and break in through the Sallyport on the Western Defences, where the Duke of Gordon and Viscount Dundee had held a clandestine meeting in March 1689. All initially went well. A sergeant and two privates serving in the castle had been bribed and the Jacobites, under Lord Drummond, prepared to make their attempt.

Under the cover of darkness, they climbed the rock face and arrived at the base of the castle walls. They had with them a ladder sufficient, so they thought, to reach over the high wall. Unfortunately, one section of the ladder was missing. The raiders decided to go ahead anyway.

What followed was sheer farce, for the ladder was indeed too short. Then the officer of the watch, making his rounds earlier than usual, saw the two colluding privates wrestling with the stunted ladder. Realising they'd been spotted, the two tried to save their own necks by throwing down the Jacobites' ropes. The ladder and everyone on it fell heavily to the rock below. Scotland's chief fortress had come perilously close to being captured.

The attempt alarmed the authorities. As a result, the artillery defences around the north and west sides were rebuilt, much as they are today. They were put to the test during the final Jacobite Rising of 1745, but only in a desultory way, for Prince Charles Edward Stuart had no heavy guns to make a serious assault. The 1745 siege proved to be the castle's last.

KINGS AND QUEENS OF SCOTLAND PART IV: HANOVERIAN

George I (1714–27)

George II (1727–60)
1730s: Castle defences largely rebuilt to their present form. 1745: The last siege of Edinburgh Castle, by Prince Charles Edward Stuart.

George III (1760–1820)
1780: A thousand prisoners of war (French, Spanish, Dutch, Irish and American) held in Edinburgh Castle. 1818: Honours of Scotland rediscovered in Crown Room by Walter Scott.

George IV (1820–30)
1822: Visits Edinburgh Castle, the first sovereign to do so in 189 years. 1829: Mons Meg returned to Edinburgh Castle from the Tower of London.

William IV (1830–37)
1830: Has the Stewart Jewels placed in the Crown Room.

Victoria (1837–1901)
1861: One o' Clock gun fired for first time. 1888: New Gatehouse built at entrance to castle.

1715

1745

JACOBITE REBELS loyal to Prince James Francis Edward Stuart ('The Old Pretender') almost recapture the castle.

PRINCE CHARLES EDWARD STUART (known as 'Bonnie Prince Charlie' or 'The Young Pretender') fails to capture the castle in what turns out to be its final siege.

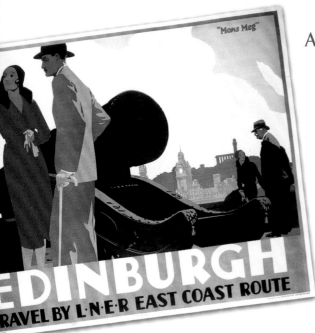

A VISITOR ATTRACTION

In February 1818, Sir Walter Scott watched as the Crown Room door was forced open. Inside he found the Honours of Scotland, exactly as they had been left in 1707, following the Treaty of Union with England. They were immediately put on public display and among the first to visit them was George IV, during a triumphal visit to Scotland in 1822. This was the first visit to the country by a reigning sovereign since Charles II in 1651.

The rediscovery of the Honours heralded a new use for the castle, as a visitor attraction. In 1829 Scott also secured the return of Mons Meg from the Tower of London, where she had been sent after the 1745 Jacobite Rising. The great gun was piped by military bands all the way from the port of Leith to her place on the battlements.

The momentum increased. In 1836, the birthchamber where James VI had been born was vacated by the army and opened to visitors. In 1846 St Margaret's Chapel was recognised among a clutter of buildings, close to where Mons Meg had been placed, and restored.

'The Regalia of Scotland will be opened for the inspection of the public in the Crown Room upon Wednesday the 26th of May instant. 150 persons only will be admitted every lawful day.'

Advertisement in the *Edinburgh Evening Courant*, 24 May 1819.

Above: A railway advertisement from around 1935 shows Mons Meg and other landmarks of Edinburgh.

> **DID YOU KNOW…**
>
> Visitors in 1819 had to pay one shilling just to view the Honours of Scotland – about £12 (€16) in today's money.

1818

SIR WALTER SCOTT rediscovers The Honours of Scotland.

1829

MONS MEG returns from 'exile' in the Tower of London.

Other more grandiose schemes were projected for the castle. Most never got off the drawing board, but several were completed, including a new Gatehouse at the main entrance in 1888, to make the castle look more like a 'real castle', and the restoration of the Great Hall in 1891.

This new role for the castle, as ancient monument and visitor attraction, was confirmed in 1905 when responsibility was transferred from the War Office to the Office of Works (now Historic Scotland).

Below: An engraving by William H. Lizars shows the grand procession marking the visit of King George IV in 1822.

KINGS AND QUEENS OF SCOTLAND PART V: SAXE-COBURG & GOTHA/WINDSOR

Edward VII (1901–10)
1905: Responsibility for Edinburgh Castle passed from War Office to Office of Works (now Historic Scotland).

George V (1910–36)
1916: One o' Clock Gun fired at a German Zeppelin bombing the city. 1927: George attends opening ceremony of Scottish National War Memorial.

Edward VIII (1936)

George VI (1936–52)
1941–5: Honours of Scotland buried in David's Tower. 1950: First performance of Edinburgh Military Tattoo on Castle Esplanade.

Elizabeth (1952–)
1953: Honours of Scotland presented to The Queen at St Giles' Cathedral, Edinburgh. 1996: Stone of Destiny returned to Edinburgh Castle. 1999: Crown of Scotland present at official opening of the Scottish Parliament – the first in 192 years.

THE CASTLE TODAY

Today the ancient royal castle is as much a powerful symbol of Scottish nationhood as it was in centuries gone by. It is an icon of Scotland's proud medieval past, the place where St Margaret of Scotland died in 1093, where James VI of Scotland and I of England was born in 1566, and where the Honours of Scotland and the Stone of Destiny – among the nation's greatest treasures – are displayed.

Edinburgh Castle has also become the spiritual home of Scotland's military history, through the presence of the Scottish National War Memorial, the National War Museum and the regimental museums of two of our great regiments, The Royal Scots and The Royal Scots Dragoon Guards. It is home also to two famous guns, medieval Mons Meg, long since silent, and the One o'Clock Gun, still very much active.

The castle has also become the home of the world-famous Edinburgh Military Tattoo. It began in 1950 as a modest event, with military bands of pipes and drums marching back and forth across the Esplanade. Now it has grown into one of the world's greatest spectacles. The castle is never more alive than in August, when the Tattoo is staged to coincide with the Edinburgh International Festival.

Above: A piper rehearsing for the Edinburgh Military Tattoo.

Opposite: The castle lit up by fireworks during the Tattoo.

DID YOU KNOW...

Edinburgh Castle welcomes well over a million visitors every year. Not bad for a fortress designed principally to keep people out!

1950

1996

THE EDINBURGH MILITARY TATTOO is staged for the first time on the Esplanade.

THE STONE OF DESTINY returns from Westminster Abbey after 700 years.

Edinburgh Castle is one of 26 Historic Scotland sites in Edinburgh and the Lothians, a selection of which is shown below.

Craigmillar Castle

Dirleton Castle and Gardens

Linlithgow Palace

Tantallon Castle

	Craigmillar Castle	Dirleton Castle and Gardens	Linlithgow Palace	Tantallon Castle
↗	2.5m (4km) SE of Edinburgh city centre, off the A7	In Dirleton village, 3m (5km) W of North Berwick on the A198	In Linlithgow, West Lothian, off the M9	3m (5km) E of North Berwick, off the A198
🕐	Open all year	Open all year	Open all year	Open all year
📞	0131 661 4445	01620 850 330	01506 842 896	01620 892 727
🚗	Approx 2.5 miles (4km) from Edinburgh Castle	Approx 25 miles (40km) from Edinburgh Castle	Approx 18 miles (30km) from Edinburgh Castle	Approx 30 miles (50km) from Edinburgh Castle

Facilities
P 🚻 🚌 🍽 🏛 ♿ 🏕 £

Facilities
P 🚌 🍽 🏛 ♿ 🏕 £

Facilities
P 🚻 🍽 🏛 🏕 £

Facilities
P 🚌 🚻 🍽 🏛 🏕 £

For more information on all Historic Scotland sites, visit **www.historic-scotland.gov.uk**
To order tickets and a wide range of gifts, visit **www.historic-scotland.gov.uk/shop**

Key to facilities

Admission charge	£
Bus/coach parking	🚌
Car parking	P
Interpretive display	🍽
Picnic area	🏕
Reasonable wheelchair access	♿
Shop	🛍
Toilets	🚻

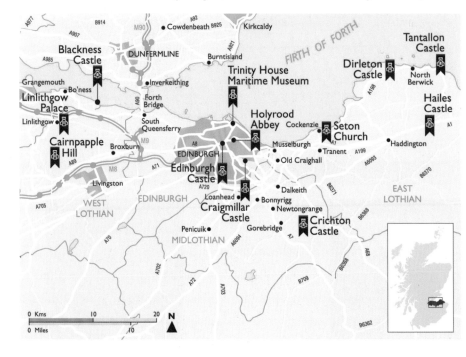